W9-BIT-825

POSTCARD

To ——————————

Love ——————————

23

Grandfathers
Are Special

GRAMERCY BOOKS
NEW YORK

This 2005 edition is published by Gramercy Books, an imprint of Random House Value Publishing, a division of Random House, Inc., New York.

Gramercy is a registered trademark and the colophon is a trademark of Random House, Inc.

Page 31, bottom quote: copyright © 1956 by Ogden Nash, reprinted by permission of Curtis Brown, Ltd.

Random House
New York • Toronto • London • Sydney • Auckland
www.randomhouse.com

Interior design: Karen Ocker Design, New York

Printed and bound in Singapore

Library of Congress Cataloging-in-Publication Data

Grandfathers are special : a tribute to those who love, lead, and inspire.
    p. cm.
    ISBN 0-517-22654-5
    1. Grandfathers—Quotations. I. Gramercy Books (Firm)

PN6084.G6G727 2005
306.874'5—dc22

2005040393

10 9 8 7 6 5 4 3 2

Grandfathers
Are Special

Grandfathers are made in heaven, born
fully formed with the birth of their first grandchild.
They are the perfect babysitters, storytellers, playmates,
and putters-to-bed. Their role is pure delight.

RUTH GOODE

Grandparents and grandchildren are
a celebration of perfection and nurturing love.

JIMMY CARTER

There are fathers who do not love their children; there
is no grandfather who does not adore his grandson.

VICTOR HUGO

Grandfather had been sitting in his old arm-chair all that
pleasant afternoon, while the children were pursuing their
various sports far off or near at hand. Sometimes you
would have said, "Grandfather is asleep;" but still, even
when his eyes were closed, his thoughts were with the
young people, playing among the flowers and shrubbery
of the garden.

NATHANIEL HAWTHORNE

Nothing makes a child smarter
than being a grandchild.

ANONYMOUS

Love is the only thing grandchildren can give you,
and the only thing you can give them.

ART BUCHWALD

The best baby-sitters, of course, are the baby's grandparents.
You feel completely comfortable entrusting your baby to them
for long periods, which is why most grandparents flee
to Florida at the earliest opportunity.

DAVE BARRY

One of life's mysteries is how the boy who wasn't
good enough to marry your daughter can be the father
of the smartest grandchild in the world.

JEWISH PROVERB

Being a daddy, with its responsibilities and chores, has made
me appreciate how much I have in common with the little
grandchildren: afternoon naps, ice cream cones, Disney
movies, early bedtimes. What a wonderful world!

BIL KEANE

Nobody can do for little children
what grandparents do.
Grandparents sort of sprinkle stardust
over the lives of little children.

ALEX HALEY

If I would have known that
grandchildren were going to be so much fun,
I would have had them first.

BILL LAURIN

The simplest toy, one which even the youngest
child can operate, is called a grandparent.

SAM LEVENSON

Surely, two of the most satisfying experiences in life
must be those of being a grandchild or a grandparent.

DONALD A. NORBERG

When I was young, my grandfather and I used to walk
around his farm. I tried desperately to step exactly into
his footprints. Now, twenty years later, I still try to follow
those footsteps. They're just different now — they are
integrity, wisdom, and love.

LISA GORMAN

What is it about grandparents that is so lovely?
I'd like to say that grandparents are God's gifts to children.
And if they can but see, hear and feel what these people
have to give, they can mature at a fast rate.

BILL COSBY

Few things are more delightful
than grandchildren fighting over your lap.

DOUG LARSON

No cowboy was ever faster on the draw than a
grandparent pulling a baby picture out of a wallet.

ANONYMOUS

They say genes skip generations.
Maybe that's why grandparents find
their grandchildren so likeable.

JOAN McINTOSH

Grandparents are our continuing tie to the near-past, to the events and beliefs and experiences that so strongly affect our lives and the world around us. Whether they are our own or surrogate grandparents who fill some of the gaps in our mobile society, our senior generation also provides our society a link to our national heritage and traditions.

We all know grandparents whose values transcend passing fads and pressures and who possess the wisdom of distilled pain and joy. Because they are usually free to love and guide and befriend the young without having to take daily responsibility for them, they can often read out past pride and fear of failure and close the space between generations.

JIMMY CARTER

Everyone needs to have access both to grandparents
and grandchildren in order to be a full human being.

MARGARET MEAD

A child needs a grandparent,
anybody's grandparent, to grow a little more
securely into an unfamiliar world.

CHARLES AND PAM MORSE

When grandparents enter the door,
discipline flies out the window.

OGDEN NASH

In the central place of every heart there is a recording chamber. So long as it receives a message of beauty, hope, cheer, and courage—so long are you young. When the wires are all down and our heart is covered with the snow of pessimism and the ice of cynicism, then, and only then, are you grown old.

DOUGLAS MACARTHUR

Have children while your parents are still young enough to take care of them.

RITA RUDNER

Perfect love sometimes does not come
till the first grandchild.

WELSH PROVERB

A grandchild will have many reasons to sound
out gladness and joy. He or she will be looking
for a special someone to send it to. Fortunate is
the grandparent who is in the right place to hear
it. Blessed is the person who answers the phone
and hears a little voice saying loudly, "I go potty."

BILL COLEMAN

FROM "PUT OFF THE WEDDING FIVE TIMES AND NOBODY COMES TO IT"

A Russian peasant…told me his grandfather
warned him:
If you ride too good a horse
you will not take the straight road to town.

CARL SANDBURG

I'll never make the mistake
of being seventy again!

CASEY STENGEL

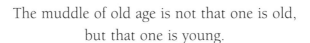

The muddle of old age is not that one is old,
but that one is young.

OSCAR WILDE

Wow! Are grandchildren great! Spoil them rotten—give them back—and laugh and laugh. Revenge is sweet.

ARIS PAINTER

Dearer than our children are the children of our children.

EGYPTIAN PROVERB

Holding a great-grandchild makes getting old worthwhile.

EVALYN RIKKERS

I am rich with years, a millionaire! I have been part of my own generation, then I watched my children's generation grow up, then my grandchildren's and now my great-grandchildren's.

DELORES GARCIA

Loving grandparents should be every infant's welcoming committee into a strange new world.

AUDREY SHERINS AND JOAN HOLLERMAN

Without doing anything spectacular, you are given your place in the great river of love that rushes underground through the generations and nourishes them.

And newborn grandchildren seem to know this in some mysterious way. They love you for nothing. They run and jump into your arms; then can be comforted and fall asleep clutching your finger or nestled against you. The aesthetic perfection of their tiny bodies is an endless consolation. Your own grey hair or crinkly arms disappear when you gaze on their shining locks and smooth skin. They give you reality. They show you the meaning of life by tumbling you into that river of love.

BETSY BLAIR

Our grandchildren accept us for ourselves, without rebuke or effort to change us, as no one in our entire lives has ever done, not our parents, siblings, spouses, friends — and hardly ever our own grown children.

RUTH GOODE

A grandparent is old on the outside but young on the inside.

ANONYMOUS

MY GRANDFATHER'S CLOCK

My grandfather's clock
was too large for the shelf
So it stood ninety years on the floor
It was taller by half than the old man himself
Though it weighed not a pennyweight more.

It was bought on the morn
Of the day that he was born
And was always his pleasure and pride
  But it stopped short
  Never to go again
When the old—man—died
  Chorus:
  Ninety years without slumbering
  Tick Tock Tick Tock
  His life seconds numbering

Tick Tock Tick
But it stopped short
Never to go again
When the old—man—died.

He watched as its pendulum rocked to and fro
Many hours he had spent as a boy
And in childhood and manhood
The clock seemed to know
And to share both his grief and his joy

For it struck twenty-four
As he entered through the door
With a blooming and beautiful bride
  But it stopped short
  Never to go again
When the old—man—died

Chorus

My Grandfather said that of those he could hire
Not a servant so faithful he found
  For it kept perfect time
  And its only desire
At the close of each week to be wound

23

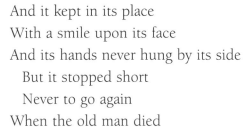

And it kept in its place
With a smile upon its face
And its hands never hung by its side
  But it stopped short
  Never to go again
When the old man died

Chorus

HENRY C. WORK

Old people are distinguished by grandchildren;
children take pride in their parents.

PROVERBS 17:6

Youth would be an ideal state if it
came a little later in life.

HERBERT ASQUITH

All would live long, but none would be old.

BENJAMIN FRANKLIN

Old age is the most unexpected of all the
things that can happen to a man.

JAMES THURBER

GRANDFATHER'S LOVE

They said he sent his love to me,
They wouldn't put it in my hand,
And when I asked them where it was
They said I couldn't understand.

I thought they must have hidden it,
I hunted for it all the day,
And when I told them so at night
They smiled and turned their heads away.

They say that love is something kind,
That I can never see or touch.
I wish he'd sent me something else,
I like his cough-drops twice as much.

Sara Teasdale

Live your life and forget your age.

NORMAN VINCENT PEALE

You've got to do your own growing, no matter how tall
your grandfather was.

IRISH PROVERB

If you want to know where I come by the passionate
commitment I have to bringing people together without
regard to race, it all started with my grandfather.

BILL CLINTON

I don't know who my grandfather was; I'm much more
concerned to know what his grandson will be.

ABRAHAM LINCOLN

Not a tenth of us who are in business are doing as well
as we could if we merely followed the principles
that were known to our grandfathers.

WILLIAM FEATHER

The great thing about baseball is when you're done, you'll
only tell your grandchildren the good things. If they ask
me about 1989, I'll tell them I had amnesia.

SPARKY ANDERSON

I don't go along with all this talk of a generation gap.
We're all contemporaries. There is only a
difference in memories, that's all.

W. H. AUDEN

Grandparents are both our past and our future.
In some ways they are what has gone before, and
in others they are what we will become.

FRED ROGERS

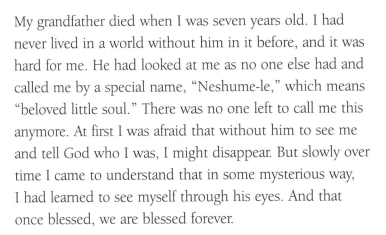

My grandfather died when I was seven years old. I had
never lived in a world without him in it before, and it was
hard for me. He had looked at me as no one else had and
called me by a special name, "Neshume-le," which means
"beloved little soul." There was no one left to call me this
anymore. At first I was afraid that without him to see me
and tell God who I was, I might disappear. But slowly over
time I came to understand that in some mysterious way,
I had learned to see myself through his eyes. And that
once blessed, we are blessed forever.

RACHEL NAOMI REMEN

I prefer to forget both pairs of glasses
and pass my declining years saluting strange
women and grandfather clocks.

OGDEN NASH

I grew up in a house where a grandfather
would greet you everyday like this, "You're eight
years old whatta ya gonna do with your life?"

BILLY CRYSTAL

I was watching the Super Bowl with my ninety-two-year-old
grandfather, and our team scored a touchdown. When
they showed the instant replay, he thought they scored
another one. I was going to tell him, but I figured the
game he was watching was better.

STEVEN WRIGHT

A child need not be very clever
To learn that "Later, dear" means "Never."

OGDEN NASH

I learned to whistle: I whistled "The Wayward Wind."
I sang "The Wayward Wind," too, at the top of my lungs
for an hour one evening, bored on the porch, hurling
myself from chair to chair singing, and wondering when
these indulgent grandparents would stop me. At length
my grandfather looked up from his paper and said,
"That's a sad song you're singing. Do you know that?"
And I was amazed he knew that. Did he yearn to
wander, my banker grandfather, like the man in
"The Wayward Wind"?

ANNIE DILLARD

Just remember, once you're over the hill
you begin to pick up speed.

CHARLES M. SCHULZ

Old age is like everything else. To make a success of it,
you've got to start young.

FRED ASTAIRE

Old age isn't so bad when you consider the alternative.

MAURICE CHEVALIER

Senescence begins
And middle age ends
The day your descendents
Outnumber your friends.

OGDEN NASH

How old would you be
if you didn't know how old you was?

LEROY "SATCHEL" PAIGE

The years between fifty and seventy are the hardest.
You are always being asked to do things, and yet you
are not decrepit enough to turn them down.

T. S. ELIOT

I'm sixty-three and I guess that puts me in with
the geriatrics, but if there were fifteen months
in every year, I'd be only forty three.

JAMES THURBER

When I was younger I could remember anything,
whether it happened or not, but I am getting old
and soon I shall remember only the latter.

MARK TWAIN

If wrinkles must be written upon our brows,
let them not be written upon the heart.
The spirit should not grow old.

JAMES A. GARFIELD

The idea is to die young as late as possible.

ASHLEY MONTAGU

There is still no cure
for the common birthday.

JOHN GLENN

To me, old age is always
fifteen years older than I am.

BERNARD BARUCH

You can't change the past, and too many folks spend their
whole lives trying to fix things that happened before their
time. You're better off using your time to improve yourself.

SADIE DELANY

How confusing the beams from memory's lamp are;
One day a bachelor, the next a grampa. What is the secret
of the trick? How did I get so old so quick?

OGDEN NASH

We are all happier in many ways when we are old than when we were young. The young sow wild oats. The old grow sage.

Winston Churchill

There aren't many of the good old days left.

Jimmy Carter

It is well known that the older a man grows, the faster he could run as a boy.

Red Smith

If you know his father and grandfather,
don't worry about his son.

AFRICAN PROVERB

Maybe you're right, boss. It all depends on the way you look at it. Look, one day I had gone to a little village. An old grandfather of ninety was busy planting an almond tree. "What, grandad!" I exclaimed. "Planting an almond tree?" and he, bent as he was, turned round and said, "My son, I carry on as if I should never die." I replied, "And I carry on as if I was going to die any minute." Which of us was right, boss?

NIKOS KAZANTZAKIS

The aging process has you firmly in its grasp
if you never get the urge to throw a snowball.

DOUG LARSON

Don't stop growing as an individual. Being a grandparent
is a new stage of life—not the final one.

CECIL B. MURPHY

My grandfather always said that living
is like licking honey off a thorn.

LOUIS ADAMIC

My grandfather once told me that there were two kinds
of people: those who do the work and those who take
the credit. He told me to try to be in the first group;
there was much less competition.

INDIRA GANDHI

Learning and love go hand in hand. My grandfather was one of those people who loved to live and loved to teach. Every time I was with him, he'd show me something about the world or something about myself that I hadn't even thought of yet. He'd help me find something wonderful in the smallest of things, and ever so carefully, he helped me understand the enormous worth of every human being.

FRED ROGERS

Every generation revolts against its fathers and makes friends with its grandfathers.

LEWIS MUMFORD

A grandparent arrives three hours early for your baptism, your graduation and your wedding because he or she wants a seat where he or she can see everything.

ERMA BOMBECK

It's one of nature's ways that we often feel closer to distant generations than to the generation immediately preceding us.

IGOR STRAVINSKY

How wonderful it would be if we could help our children and grandchildren to learn thanksgiving at an early age. Thanksgiving opens the doors. It changes a child's personality. A child is resentful, negative—or thankful. Thankful children want to give, they radiate happiness, they draw people.

SIR JOHN TEMPLETON

When you teach your son,
you teach your son's son.

THE TALMUD

A good man leaves an inheritance
to his children's children.

PROVERBS 13:22A

Actor David Carradine, son of John Carradine, said
in gratitude of his father's accomplishments, "I could
stand on his shoulders and feel twice as tall." That each
generation could stand on the shoulders of the last and
feel twice as tall is a poetic hope for all our families.

FRED ROGERS

Give a little love to a child
and you get a great deal back.

JOHN RUSKIN

A baby is God's opinion
that life should go on.

CARL SANDBURG

I'm going to ask something of every one of you. Now let
me start with my generation, with the grandparents out
there. You are our living link with the past. Tell your
grandchildren the story of struggles waged at home and
abroad, of sacrifices freely made for freedom's sake. And
tell them your own story as well, because every American
has a story to tell.

GEORGE H. W. BUSH

As we peer into society's future, we—you
and I, and our government—must avoid the
impulse to live only for today, plundering
for our own ease and convenience, the precious
resources of tomorrow. We cannot mortgage
the material assets of our grandchildren without
asking the loss also of their political and
spiritual heritage. We want democracy to
survive for all generations to come, not to
become the insolvent phantom of tomorrow.

DWIGHT D. EISENHOWER

The closest friends I have made all through life have
been people who also grew up close to a loved
and living grandmother or grandfather.

MARGARET MEAD

You can't help getting older,
but you don't have to get old.

GEORGE BURNS

And in the end, it's not the years in your life
that count. It's the life in your years.

ABRAHAM LINCOLN

When you're pushing seventy, that's enough.

ANONYMOUS

Grandchildren don't make a man feel old; it's the knowledge that he's married to a grandmother.

G. Norman Collie

There is nothing which for my part I like better... than conversing with aged men; for I regard them as travelers who have gone a journey which I too may have to go, and of whom I ought to inquire, whether the way is smooth and easy, or rugged and difficult.

Plato

Like everyone else who makes the mistake of getting older, I begin each day with coffee and obituaries.

Bill Cosby

Age is a question of mind over matter.
If you don't mind, it doesn't matter.

LEROY "SATCHEL" PAIGE

I would enthusiastically recommend to any friend
or colleague the wonderful sport of grandparenting.
It can be as simple or as elaborate as you care to make it.
It can involve physical or mental games. But in the
final analysis, it is an activity of the heart.

DOUG DAFT

Being grandparents sufficiently removes us from the
responsibilities so that we can be friends.

ALLAN FROME

45

Grandparents aren't better than parents.
Children know that. But grandparents are definitely
different. They have more secret compartments, more smiles,
and more time to listen. At least it seems that way. There is
just something magical about being a grandparent.

BILL COLEMAN

An only daughter and numerous family of grandchildren,
will furnish me great resources of happiness.

THOMAS JEFFERSON

By the time the youngest children have learned
to keep the house tidy, the oldest grandchildren
are on hand to tear it to pieces.

CHRISTOPHER MORLEY

RALPH WALDO EMERSON TO HIS DAUGHTER EDITH, ON THE BIRTH OF A GRANDSON, JULY 11, 1866

My dear Edith,

Happy wife and Mother that you are — and not the less surely that the birth of your babe touches this old house and its people and neighbors with unusual joy. I hope the best gifts and graces of his father and mother will combine for this blossom, and highest influences hallow and ripen the firm and perfect fruit. There is nothing in this world so serious as the advent of a child with all his possibilities to parents with good minds and hearts. Fair fall the little boy — he has come among good people. . . . I please myself already that his Fortunes will be worthy of these great days of his country, that he will not be frivolous, that he will be noble and true, and will know what is sacred. . . .

Your loving father,

R.W. EMERSON

A friend of mine was asked how she liked having her first
great-grandchild. "It was wonderful," she replied, "until
I suddenly realized that I was the mother of a grandfather!"

ROBERT L RICE, M.D.

If you see a book, a rocking chair, and a grandchild
in the same room, don't pass up the chance to read
aloud. Instill in your grandchild a love of reading.
It's one of the greatest gifts that you can give.

BARBARA BUSH

It's funny what happens when you become
a grandparent. You start to act all goofy and do things
you never thought you'd do. It's terrific.

MIKE KRZYZEWSKI

A grandparent pretends he doesn't
know who you are on Halloween.

ERMA BOMBECK

Always remember, being the grandfather means having
the most fun and bearing the least responsibility of all the
relatives of the baby, and you'll see, by not bothering them
about their dirty underwear, and scraping the food off their
face with a spoon, you'll be the one they love most.

SAUL TURTELTAUB

The birth of a grandchild is a wonderful and exciting event!
That wonder and excitement continues throughout life.

TOM POTTS

I do love being a grandfather, and I wonder if it
wasn't because my Grandfather McFeely loved me
so much, and I had such a good time with him.

FRED ROGERS

Elephants and grandchildren never forget.

ANDY ROONEY

Grandma and Grandpa, tell me a story and snuggle me
with your love. When I'm in your arms, the world seems
small and we're blessed by the heavens above.

LAURA SPIESS

Our children are here to stay, but our babies and toddlers and preschoolers are gone as fast as they can grow up— and we have only a short moment with each. When you see a grandfather take a baby in his arms, you see that the moment hasn't always been long enough.

St. Clair Adams Sullivan

Don't ever, ever underestimate the will of a grandfather. We're madmen. We don't give a damn. We got here before you, and they'll be here after. We'll make enemies, we'll break laws, we'll break bones. But you will not mess with the grandchildren.

The West Wing's Jed Bartlet

I worked as a chief business executive for over 40 years. I made major decisions. I worked side by side with powerful men and women. But one grandchild has changed me more than any of those people I worked with, and I have learned more from watching my children be parents than I learned in all those 40 years in the workplace.

ANONYMOUS

Never have children, only grandchildren.

GORE VIDAL

Old Man: You get old and you can't do
             anybody any good any more.
Boy: You do me some good, Grandpa.
             You tell me things.

ROBERT PENN WARREN

The joy of interacting with grandchildren is
a bonus none of us deserves, but how fortunate
we are that God sent these gifts along.

BILL AND PAT COLEMAN

From time to time, I've learned to take a troubled
grandchild and look him or her squarely in the eye
in a private setting and just simply say, "You are not
only my grandchild, you are a child of God. You
have infinite worth. You have divine potential. You
are not to compare yourself to anyone else. You are
precious in your own right. I believe in you and love
you with all the heart." I've often had a grandchild
respond, "Would you please say that again?"

STEPHEN COVEY

To show a child what had once delighted you,
to find the child's delight added to your own, so that
there is now a double delight seen in the glow
of trust and affection, this is happiness.

J. B. PRIESTLY

You don't think it's possible to love your
grandchildren any more than you do today...
but then tomorrow comes.

ANONYMOUS

May you live to enjoy your grandchildren.

PSALM 128:6A

A grandparent can always be counted on to buy all your cookies, flower seeds, all-purpose greeting cards, transparent tape, paring knives, peanut brittle and ten chances on a pony. (Also a box of taffy when they have dentures.)

Erma Bombeck

There is no woman more precious than the daughter who will not allow her father to change her child's diaper.

Saul Turteltaub

What children need most are the essentials that grandparents provide in abundance. They give unconditional love, kindness, patience, humor, comfort, lessons in life. And, most importantly, cookies.

Rudolph W. Giuliani

FROM "THE CENTENARIAN"

Great Grandfather was ninety-nine
   And so it was our one dread,
That though his health was superfine
   He'd fail to make the hundred.
Though he was not a rolling stone
   No moss he seemed to gather:
A patriarch of brawn and bone
         Was Great Grandfather.

ROBERT WILLIAM SERVICE

The young don't know what age is, and
the old forget what youth was.

SEAMUS MACMANUS

For the unlearned, old age is winter; for the learned,
it is the season of the harvest.

HASIDIC PROVERB

Winter is on my head, but spring is in my heart.

VICTOR HUGO

Our greatest responsibility
is to be good ancestors.

JONAS SALK

I don't know that I'll be alive when my grandsons have children, and so they just may be the last Rogerses that I'm acquainted with on this earth. I know they will have lots inside of them to give to their children or nieces or nephews. But still, it is really fun for me to see them doing things that I know Rogerses have done for a long, long time. There is a continuity that goes through the generations. My friend and teacher, Dr. Margaret McFarland, used to say, "I love being part of the beach of life—I like being one of the grains of sand."

FRED ROGERS

Stop thinking your grandchildren will be
OK no matter how wasteful or destructive
you may be, since they can go to a
nice new planet on a spaceship.

KURT VONNEGUT

Is it possible that we—we Americans, we Soviets, we humans—are at last coming to our senses and beginning to work together on behalf of the species and the planet? Nothing is promised. History has placed this burden on our shoulders. It is up to us to build a future worthy of our children and grandchildren.

CARL SAGAN

Our children are not going to be just "our children"
—they are going to be other people's husbands and
wives and the parents of our grandchildren.

MARY S. CALDERONE

We must protect the forests for our children, grandchildren
and children yet to be born. We must protect the forests
for those who can't speak for themselves such
as the birds, animals, fish and trees.

CHIEF EDWARD MOODY

Our greatest obligation to our children and grandchildren
is to prepare them to understand and to deal effectively
with the world in which they will live—not with the world
we have known or the world we would prefer to have.

GRAYSON KIRK

What a wonderful contribution our grandmothers and
grandfathers can make if they will share some of the rich
experiences and their testimonies with their children and
grandchildren.

VAUGHN J. FEATHERSTONE

Each generation, in its turn, is a link between all that has gone before and all that comes after. That is true genetically, and it is equally true in the transmission of identity. Our parents gave us what they were able to give, and we took what we could of it and made it part of ourselves. If we knew our grandparents, and even great-grandparents, we will have taken from them what they could offer us, too. All that helped to make us who we are. We, in our turn, will offer what we can of ourselves to our children and their offspring.

FRED ROGERS

Too old to plant trees for my own gratification,
I shall do it for my posterity.

THOMAS JEFFERSON

Before my grandfather died, he bought a trellis and trained the roses to weave slowly up both sides and join together at the top in an embrace, completing the purpose of the trellis and fulfilling my grandfather's desire to leave something behind.

CHRISTOPHER DE VINCK

Even if I knew that tomorrow the world would go to pieces, I would still plant my apple tree.

MARTIN LUTHER KING, JR.

One generation plants the trees; another gets the shade.

CHINESE PROVERB

Treat the earth well; it was not given to you by your parents, it was loaned to you by your children. We do not inherit the Earth from our ancestors, we borrow it from our children.

NATIVE AMERICAN PROVERB

You can't do much about your ancestors,
but you can influence your descendents enormously.
Toil, feel, think, hope; you will be sure to dream enough
before you die, without arranging for it.

J. STERLING

63

For grandparents, now is the time to live. All that has gone before has been largely preparation—one has discharged his or her obligations, made his or her contribution to society, founded a home, raised a family, and now the ultimate goal, life itself, is at hand.

HOWARD WHITMAN

The mental image of a loving grandfather may be a piece
of the picture that his grandchildren carry to maturity as
a part of their concept of godliness. What an opportunity!
What a gift! What a responsibility! Oh, that I can make
a difference, an eternal difference, in the lives of children.

DAVID BOOTH

The presence of a grandparent confirms that parents were,
indeed, little once, too, and that people who are little can
grow to be big, can become parents, and one day even
have grandchildren of their own. So often we think of
grandparents as belonging to the past; but in this important
way, grandparents, for young children, belong to the future.

FRED ROGERS